MASTER
THE FUTURE OF
HOME BUSINESS

A 22nd Century Blueprint

Are you feeling overwhelmed by the rapidly changing business landscape? Need help balancing work and home life in this tech-driven era? "22nd Century Home Business Strategy Blueprint" is your essential guide to navigating and thriving in the modern world of home-based businesses. This book is a beacon for entrepreneurs and home business aspirants who seek to make their mark in the 21st century and beyond.

ABOUT THIS BOOK

- **Cutting-Edge Strategies**: Discover innovative methods tailored for the 22nd century, helping you stay ahead in a competitive market.
- **Balancing Work and Life**: Learn practical techniques to maintain a healthy work-life balance in a home business setting.
- **Technology Integration**: Explore how to harness the latest technological advancements to streamline your business operations.
- **Networking and Brand Building**: Understand the art of building a robust network and a powerful brand from the comfort of your home.
- **Financial Planning and Management**: Get insights into efficient financial strategies for maximizing profits and minimizing risks.
- **Sustainable Growth Models**: Uncover sustainable business models that promise long-term growth and stability.

- **Real-Life Success Stories**: Be inspired by stories of individuals who have successfully transitioned to and prospered in home-based businesses.

Step into the future with confidence. Whether planning to start a new home business or revitalize your existing one, the "22nd Century Home Business Strategy Blueprint" is your key to success. Embrace the future of home-based business and transform your entrepreneurial dreams into reality. **Get your copy today!**

Cutting-Edge Strategies: Staying Ahead in a Competitive Market

In the fast-paced and ever-evolving landscape of the 22nd century, staying ahead in the business world requires a keen understanding of cutting-edge strategies. "22nd Century Home Business Strategy Blueprint" delves into innovative methods that are tailor-made for navigating the complexities of modern markets. Here's a glimpse of what you can expect from this crucial section of the book:

- **Leveraging Emerging Technologies**: The book emphasizes integrating emerging technologies like artificial intelligence, blockchain, and the

Internet of Things (IoT) into your business practices. This streamlines operations and provides a competitive edge through enhanced efficiency and innovative services or products.

- **Adaptive Business Models**: Learn about flexible and adaptive business models that can swiftly respond to market changes and consumer demands. This section discusses the significance of agility in business planning and execution, allowing you to stay relevant and competitive.

- **Data-Driven Decision Making**: In an era where data is king, understanding how to effectively gather, analyze, and utilize data can make a significant difference. The book guides you through the process of using data analytics to make informed decisions, predict market trends, and personalize customer experiences.

- **Sustainable Practices**: Embracing sustainability is not just about being environmentally conscious; it's also a strategic business decision. This part explores how adopting sustainable practices can lead to cost savings, improve brand image, and open new market opportunities.

- **Remote Workforce Management**: With the rise of remote working, learn effective strategies for managing a distributed workforce. This includes leveraging digital collaboration tools, fostering a robust remote work culture, and ensuring productivity and engagement among team members.

- **Digital Marketing and Social Media Mastery**: Understand the nuances of digital marketing and social media in the 21st century. This includes strategies for building a solid online presence, engaging with your audience, and leveraging digital platforms for brand growth and customer acquisition.

- **Innovative Financing Options**: Explore new and innovative ways to finance your business, from crowdfunding and peer-to-peer lending to leveraging digital currencies and tokenization.

These strategies are designed to help you survive and thrive in a competitive market. With "22nd Century Home Business Strategy Blueprint," you are equipped with the knowledge and tools to build a resilient, forward-thinking, and successful home business prepared for the challenges and opportunities of the 22nd century.

CONTENTS

INTRODUCTION

The Evolving Landscape of Home Business

In the luminous dawn of the 22nd century, the concept of 'home business' has evolved far beyond its quaint, 20th-century origins. Once seen as a mere sideline or a humble start-up approach, it has blossomed into our global economy's central pillar. This transformation has not been a simple change but a radical reinvention.

Gone are the days when geographical boundaries, technological constraints, and a lack of resources limited home businesses. Today, they stand at the forefront of innovation, harnessing the boundless potential of digital landscapes and global connectivity. We have witnessed a paradigm shift from traditional brick-and-mortar establishments to dynamic, virtual enterprises operating seamlessly in the ever-expanding digital cosmos.

This metamorphosis was not just a technological revolution but also a cultural one. Integrating advanced technologies like artificial intelligence, blockchain, and the Internet of Things (IoT) into our daily business practices has redefined what we sell, how we sell it, and who we are as entrepreneurs, innovators, and dreamers. We have transcended the mere act of selling goods and services; we are now architects of experiences, digital content curators, and pioneers on the digital frontier.

In this brave new world, adaptation is not just a strategy but a necessity. Those who thrive are not merely the ones with the most robust financial backing or the latest gadgets; they are the ones who can dance to the rhythm of a rapidly changing landscape. They are adaptable, resilient, and ever-evolving – just like the market they inhabit.

As we enter this uncharted territory, the "22nd Century Home Business Strategy Blueprint" emerges as your compass and guide. This book is not just a collection of strategies and tips. It is a beacon, illuminating the path to success in an age where change is the only constant. It invites you to join the vanguard of this new era: to embrace the unknown, harness the potential of the 22nd century, and redefine the essence of what it means to run a home business.

Welcome to the future of entrepreneurship. Welcome to the revolution of home business in the 22nd century.

Chapter 1

UNDERSTANDING THE 22ND-CENTURY MARKET

Key Market Trends and Predictions

As we journey through the 22nd century, the market landscape presents a kaleidoscope of emerging trends and predictions shaping business's future. The dawn of this century has seen the rise of decentralized markets, the explosion of virtual reality (VR) and augmented reality (AR) based commerce, and the increasing significance of sustainable and ethical business practices. In this vibrant milieu, businesses must navigate the wave of digital currencies and blockchain technology, redefining the nature of financial transactions and data security.

The gig economy continues to burgeon, powered by an ever-evolving freelance workforce that values flexibility and autonomy. This shift has profound implications for home businesses, which are now positioned at the forefront of this transformation. Furthermore, integrating AI and machine learning in everyday business operations is a luxury and necessary to stay competitive and predictive in this dynamic market.

The Role of Technology in Business Evolution

Technology has been the centrifugal force in the evolution of the 22nd-century marketplace. The advent of AI and machine learning has given rise to predictive analytics, revolutionizing how businesses anticipate consumer needs and market trends. The proliferation of IoT devices has turned homes into interconnected business hubs, enabling entrepreneurs to operate with unprecedented efficiency and scalability.

Blockchain technology is no longer just a buzzword; it's a foundational element in ensuring transparency and security in business operations. The rise of 5G networks has facilitated lightning-fast communication and data transfer, making remote business operations more feasible and efficient.

In this digital era, businesses integrating these technological advancements must catch up. Technology is an enabler and a critical driver of business growth, innovation, and sustainability in the 22nd century.

Consumer Behavior in the Digital Age

Understanding consumer behavior in the digital age is akin to navigating a complex web of digital footprints. The modern consumer is more informed, connected, and socially conscious. The impact of social media on consumer choices is profound, with peer reviews and influencer marketing playing a significant role in purchasing decisions.

Personalization has become the cornerstone of consumer engagement. Businesses that harness data to offer personalized experiences are more likely to win customer loyalty. Moreover, there is a growing trend towards experiential commerce where consumers seek immersive and interactive shopping experiences, often blending the physical and digital worlds.

The rise of ethical consumerism has also prompted businesses to adopt more sustainable and socially responsible practices. Consumers increasingly align their purchasing power with their values, making corporate social responsibility a vital component of any business strategy.

In conclusion, the 22nd-century market is a dynamic and ever-evolving entity. By understanding these key trends and adapting to the changing role of technology and consumer behavior, home businesses can survive and thrive in this exciting new era of commerce. This chapter lays the foundation for the strategies and insights explored in the subsequent chapters, each designed to equip you with the knowledge and tools to excel in the 22nd-century marketplace.

Chapter 2

SETTING UP YOUR HOME BUSINESS

Choosing the Right Business Model

In the tapestry of the 22nd century's business landscape, selecting the appropriate business model is akin to choosing the right thread to weave your success. This section delves into various contemporary business models suitable for a home-based setup. From traditional sole proprietorships to modern digital models like dropshipping, affiliate marketing, and subscription services, we explore the pros and cons of each. The chapter also discusses hybrid models that blend online and offline elements, catering to the diverse needs of today's market. Crucially, we address how to align your business model with your personal goals, market demand, and the scalability potential to ensure long-term success.

Essential Tools and Technology for Home Businesses

The right tools and technology are the lifeblood of any 22nd-century home business. This part of the chapter is a comprehensive guide to the essential technological arsenal for modern entrepreneurs. We cover the basics, like high-speed internet, cloud computing services, and cybersecurity measures to protect your digital assets. The chapter introduces advanced tools such as AI-based customer relationship management (CRM) systems, virtual reality (VR) for product demonstrations, and blockchain for secure transactions. Emphasis is placed on how these tools can optimize operations, enhance customer experiences, and keep your business ahead in a technology-driven market.

Creating a Productive Home Office Environment

Your home office is more than just a physical space; it's the command center of your business. This segment focuses on creating an environment that fosters productivity, creativity, and wellness. We begin with the basics of ergonomic furniture and practical workspace layout. The chapter then explores integrating smart home technology for efficient workspace management, including automated lighting, temperature control, and noise-cancellation systems. Furthermore, we discuss the importance of separating work from personal life when your office is home, offering practical tips on maintaining this balance. Lastly, the role of mental and physical well-being is highlighted, suggesting ways to create a space that boosts productivity and supports your overall health.

In this chapter, "Setting Up Your Home Business," we provide a roadmap to navigate through the initial phase of your entrepreneurial journey. Each section is designed to equip you with the knowledge, tools, and insights needed to lay a solid foundation for your home business in the 22nd century.

Roadmap for Navigating the Initial Phase of Your 22nd Century Home Business Journey

Embarking on an entrepreneurial journey in the 22nd century can be exhilarating yet daunting. This roadmap is designed to guide you through the initial stages, equipping you with essential knowledge, tools, insights, and unique hacks to establish a solid foundation for your home business.

1. Identify Your Niche and Business Model

- **Knowledge**: Research market trends and identify gaps where your skills and interests align with consumer needs.
- **Hack**: Use data analytics and social media listening tools to identify emerging trends and underserved markets.
- **Tool**: Utilize online market research platforms to gather comprehensive insights.

2. Develop a Business Plan

- **Knowledge**: Understand the components of a solid business plan, including market analysis, financial projections, and strategic objectives.
- **Hack**: Leverage business plan software with templates and guides for home businesses.
- **Tool**: Online business plan builders and financial modeling tools.

3. Set Up Your Legal Framework

- **Knowledge**: Familiarize yourself with legal requirements, such as business registration, licenses, and tax obligations.
- **Hack**: Consult online legal services for affordable advice and document preparation.
- **Tool**: Digital legal assistance platforms and automated tax software.

4. Embrace Technology and Digital Tools

- **Knowledge**: Understand the importance of technology in streamlining operations, marketing, and customer engagement.

- **Hack**: Use AI-powered tools for customer service and marketing automation.
- **Tool**: CRM software, social media management tools, and cloud computing services.

5. Create a Productive Home Office

- **Knowledge**: Learn about efficient and ergonomic home office setup elements.
- **Hack**: Implement smart home technologies for efficient energy use and enhanced productivity.
- **Tool**: Ergonomic furniture, noise-canceling headphones, and intelligent lighting.

6. Build Your Online Presence

- **Knowledge**: Recognize the importance of a solid online presence in reaching and engaging customers.
- **Hack**: Optimize your website for search engines and leverage social media advertising.
- **Tool**: Website building platforms, SEO tools, and social media analytics.

7. Network and Collaborate

- **Knowledge**: Understand the power of networking and collaboration in expanding your business reach.
- **Hack**: Join online forums and virtual trade shows to connect with peers and potential partners.
- **Tool**: Professional networking platforms and virtual event software.

8. Plan for Financial Management

- **Knowledge**: Grasp the basics of financial management, including budgeting, cash flow management, and investment strategies.
- **Hack**: Utilize financial management software with predictive analytics for better financial planning.
- **Tool**: Budgeting tools, digital bookkeeping software, and investment tracking apps.

9. Foster Continuous Learning and Adaptation

- **Knowledge**: Stay abreast of market changes and technological advancements.

- **Hack**: Subscribe to industry newsletters, attend webinars, and participate in online courses.
- **Tool**: E-learning platforms and digital subscriptions to industry publications.

10. Focus on Customer Experience

By following this roadmap, you will understand what it takes to start and grow a successful home business in the 22nd century. Each step is designed to build upon the last, ensuring you are well-prepared to meet the challenges and seize the opportunities of this exciting new era of entrepreneurship.

Chapter 3

CUTTING-EDGE STRATEGIES FOR SUCCESS

Innovative Marketing and Branding Techniques

In the digital tapestry of the 22nd century, marketing and branding have transcended traditional boundaries, evolving into a realm of limitless creativity and innovation. This section delves into pioneering marketing strategies that leverage the latest digital tools and platforms. We explore the power of immersive technologies like augmented reality (AR) and virtual reality (VR) in creating engaging brand experiences. A solid online presence is emphasized, with insights into successful social media strategies, influencer partnerships, and content marketing tactics that resonate with a digitally savvy audience.

Focus is given to personalization and customization in marketing, harnessing the power of AI to deliver tailored messages and experiences to individual consumers. The chapter also covers the art of storytelling in branding, illustrating how a compelling narrative can foster a deep, emotional connection with your target audience, turning customers into brand advocates.

Leveraging Data and Analytics

Data is the new currency in the 22nd-century marketplace, and its intelligent use is critical to business success. This chapter focuses on effectively gathering, analyzing, and utilizing data to drive business decisions. We discuss implementing advanced analytics tools to understand market trends, consumer behavior, and operational efficiencies.

The chapter also covers predictive analytics, a tool that provides insights into current patterns and forecasts future trends, allowing businesses to stay ahead of the curve. The ethical considerations and privacy concerns associated with data collection and analysis are also addressed, ensuring businesses maintain trust and integrity in their operations.

Adopting Sustainable Business Practices

Sustainability is no longer just an environmental concern; it's a business imperative. This section highlights the importance of integrating sustainable practices into every aspect of your business. We explore eco-friendly business models and practices that benefit the environment and enhance brand reputation and customer loyalty.

Topics include sustainable materials sourcing, energy-efficient operations, and waste reduction strategies. The chapter also discusses the growing trend of social entrepreneurship and how businesses can contribute to societal well-being while achieving economic success. Finally, we delve into the circular economy concept and its role in fostering long-term sustainability in business practices.

In this chapter, "Cutting-Edge Strategies for Success," you are introduced to a suite of modern strategies and practices essential for the success of a 22nd-century home business. From innovative marketing techniques to the prudent use of data and adopting sustainable practices, this chapter provides a comprehensive guide to staying ahead in a rapidly evolving business landscape.

A. Predictive Analytics: Gaining a Competitive Edge

Understanding Predictive Analytics

Predictive analytics involves using data, statistical algorithms, and machine learning techniques to identify the likelihood of future outcomes based on historical data. This means anticipating market trends, customer behaviors, and potential business operational challenges before they become evident. It allows for proactive decision-making, ensuring companies stay ahead of their competitors by adapting to changes more swiftly and efficiently.

The Edge Offered by Predictive Analytics

- **Anticipating Market Trends**: Businesses can identify patterns and trends likely to reoccur by analyzing past market data. This insight can guide product development, marketing strategies, and inventory management.
- **Understanding Consumer Behavior**: Predictive analytics helps segment customers based on buying patterns, preferences, and behaviors, allowing for more targeted and effective marketing campaigns.
- **Optimizing Operations**: Through predictive maintenance, businesses can foresee potential equipment failures or operational bottlenecks, reducing downtime and improving overall efficiency.
- **Risk Management**: Predictive models can assess risks in investment, credit lending, and even day-to-day operating activities, enabling better risk mitigation strategies.

Ethical Considerations and Privacy Concerns

The use of predictive analytics raises significant ethical and privacy concerns, particularly regarding data collection and usage:

- **Data Privacy**: Businesses must ensure that the data collected for predictive analytics complies with all relevant data protection laws, like GDPR. Customers should be informed about what data is being collected and how it will be used.

- **Consent**: Obtaining explicit consent from individuals before ordering and using their data is crucial. Users should have the option to opt out of data collection.

- **Bias and Fairness**: Predictive models can unintentionally perpetuate biases if the historical data is biased. It's vital to regularly audit and update these models to ensure fairness and objectivity.

- **Transparency**: Businesses should be transparent about their use of predictive analytics. This includes being open about the kind of predictions being made and how they influence business decisions.

Analytics Tools for Business Insights

Several analytics tools are pivotal in understanding market trends, consumer behavior, and operational efficiencies:

- **Customer Relationship Management (CRM) Systems**: These systems integrate data analytics to provide insights into customer preferences and behaviors, enhancing customer service and engagement.
- **Supply Chain Analytics Tools**: These tools help predict inventory needs, manage supply chain disruptions, and optimize logistics.
- **Financial Analytics Software**: Such software assists in budget forecasting, revenue prediction, and financial risk assessment.
- **Social Media Analytics Tools**: These tools analyze social media trends and consumer sentiments, offering valuable insights into brand perception and market trends.

In conclusion, predictive analytics offers businesses in the 22nd century an unparalleled advantage in understanding and adapting to market dynamics. However, this power comes with ensuring ethical practices and respecting customer privacy. By balancing these aspects, businesses can harness the full potential of predictive analytics to stay competitive and responsive in a rapidly evolving market.

B. The Imperative of Integrating Sustainable Practices in Business

In the 22nd century, sustainability is no longer a buzzword or an optional add-on for businesses; it's a fundamental aspect of successful and responsible operations. Integrating sustainable practices into every facet of a business is crucial for several reasons:

Environmental Responsibility

- **Resource Efficiency**: Sustainable practices often involve using resources more efficiently, reducing waste, and minimizing environmental impact. This can include everything from energy-efficient office equipment to eco-friendly manufacturing processes.

- **Reducing Carbon Footprint**: Implementing green initiatives such as using renewable energy sources and adopting low-carbon technologies helps lessen a business's carbon footprint, a vital step in combating climate change.

Enhancing Brand Reputation and Customer Loyalty

- **Brand Differentiation**: A commitment to sustainability can set a business apart in a crowded market. Consumers are increasingly environmentally conscious and tend to favor brands that are committed to eco-friendly practices.
- **Building Trust**: Transparency in sustainable practices builds trust with customers and stakeholders. This trust translates into customer loyalty, as consumers are more likely to support brands that share their values of environmental stewardship.

- **Attracting Eco-conscious Consumers**: A growing market segment consists of consumers prioritizing sustainability in their purchasing decisions. Businesses that adopt green practices are more likely to attract and retain these consumers.

Eco-Friendly Business Models and Practices

- **Circular Economy Models**: Moving away from the traditional linear economy of 'take-make-dispose,' circular economy models focus on reusing, recycling, and refurbishing to create a closed-loop system. This reduces waste and encourages the sustainable use of resources.
- **Green Supply Chain Management**: Implementing eco-friendly practices throughout the supply chain, from sustainable sourcing of raw materials to green logistics and packaging solutions.
- **Sustainable Products and Services**: Developing products and services that are eco-friendly in their production and encourage

sustainable usage among consumers. Examples include biodegradable products, energy-saving devices, and services that promote environmental conservation.

- **Energy-Efficient Operations**: Adopting energy-efficient technologies and practices in the workplace, such as LED lighting, energy-efficient appliances, and intelligent building systems to reduce energy consumption.

- **Environmental Certifications and Standards Compliance**: Obtaining certifications like LEED, Energy Star, or ISO 14001 ensures compliance with environmental standards and signals a commitment to sustainability to consumers and partners.

- **Employee Engagement in Sustainability**: Fostering a culture of sustainability within the organization by involving employees in green initiatives, sustainability training, and eco-friendly workplace practices.

- **Community and Environmental Outreach**: Engaging in community-based environmental projects and initiatives demonstrating a commitment to ecological well-being beyond business operations.

By integrating these sustainable practices into every aspect of their business, companies contribute positively to the environment, enhance their brand reputation, and deepen customer loyalty. In the long run, these practices lead to sustainable business growth and a stronger connection with a customer base that values and supports eco-conscious businesses.

C. Expanding on Sustainable Business Practices

Sustainable Sourcing of Materials

Sustainable sourcing involves procuring materials in a way that is environmentally friendly and socially responsible. This means choosing suppliers who adhere to eco-friendly practices, such as using renewable resources, minimizing chemical usage, and ensuring fair labor practices. By integrating sustainable sourcing into their operations, businesses reduce their environmental impact and support ethical supply chains. This approach can enhance brand value and customer loyalty, as consumers are increasingly aware of and concerned about the origins of the products they purchase.

Energy-Efficient Operations

Energy efficiency in business operations is crucial for reducing environmental impact and cutting costs. This can be achieved through various means:

- **Upgrading to Energy-Efficient Equipment**: Using appliances and machines that consume less energy without compromising performance.
- **Smart Building Solutions**: Implementing smart thermostats, efficient lighting systems, and sensor-based controls to minimize energy waste.
- **Renewable Energy Sources**: Investing in renewable energy sources like solar, wind, or geothermal to power business operations.

Waste Reduction Strategies

Waste reduction is a critical component of sustainable business practices. Strategies include:

- **Recycling and Reusing**: Implementing comprehensive recycling programs and finding ways to reuse materials in the production process.
- **Minimizing Packaging**: Using minimal and eco-friendly packaging encourages customers to recycle or reuse packaging.
- **Digitalization**: Moving towards paperless operations and digital processes to reduce paper waste.

Social Entrepreneurship: Contributing to Societal Well-Being

Social entrepreneurship represents a growing trend where businesses are focused on profitability and generating positive societal impact. This can be achieved in several ways:

- **Solving Social Issues**: Developing products or services that address societal challenges such as poverty, education, health, and environmental conservation.

- **Ethical Business Practices**: Operating in a manner that is fair, ethical, and beneficial to society, including acceptable labor practices and community engagement.
- **Investing in the Community**: Contributing a portion of profits to social causes or engaging in community development projects.

Balancing Profit and Purpose

The key for businesses in the 22nd century is to find the balance between achieving economic success and contributing to societal well-being. This balance can be achieved by:

- **Integrating Social Goals into Business Objectives**: Making societal impact a core part of the business strategy, not just a side activity.
- **Measuring Impact**: Regularly assessing business activities' social and environmental impact and adjusting as necessary.

- **Engaging Stakeholders**: Involving customers, employees, and the community in sustainable and socially responsible initiatives, creating a sense of shared purpose and commitment.

In conclusion, integrating sustainable practices into every aspect of a business, from sourcing materials to operations and waste management, is crucial in the 22nd century. Furthermore, embracing the concept of social entrepreneurship allows businesses to play a significant role in societal well-being while achieving economic success. This holistic approach to business meets the demands of a modern, conscious consumer base and paves the way for a more sustainable and equitable future.

The Circular Economy: Fostering Long-Term Sustainability in Business

The circular economy represents a paradigm shift from the traditional linear 'take, make, dispose' model to a more sustainable and efficient system. This concept is pivotal in fostering long-term sustainability in business practices, particularly in the 22nd century, where resource conservation and environmental impact are at the forefront of business considerations.

Understanding the Circular Economy

The circular economy is based on three fundamental principles:

- **Design Out Waste and Pollution**: It begins at the design stage, where products are created to be used and reused as much as possible, minimizing waste and pollution.
- **Keep Products and Materials in Use**: This principle focuses on maintaining the value of products and materials for as long as possible through reuse, repair, remanufacturing, and recycling. It contrasts sharply with the linear model, where products are disposed of after use.
- **Regenerate Natural Systems**: In a circular economy, the aim is to enhance natural systems rather than exploit them, for example, by returning valuable nutrients to the soil to support regeneration.

Role in Business Practices

Incorporating the circular economy into business practices involves several vital approaches:

- **Product Life Extension**: Designing products for durability and ease of maintenance, repair, and upgrade. This extends the product's life cycle and reduces the need for new resources.
- **Resource Recovery**: Implementing processes to recover and reuse materials at the end of a product's life, thus reducing waste and the demand for virgin materials.
- **Service and Sharing Models**: Transitioning from selling products to providing services, such as sharing platforms or leasing models. This encourages efficient use of resources and reduces waste.
- **Sustainable Supply Chains**: Building supply chains supporting circular practices, such as sourcing recycled materials and working with suppliers who adhere to circular principles.
- **Eco-Design**: Designing products with their entire lifecycle in mind, considering factors like recyclability and energy efficiency during the manufacturing and usage phases.

Benefits for Businesses

The circular economy offers several benefits for businesses:

- **Cost Savings**: Reduced material costs and waste lead to significant savings. Efficient resource use and waste reduction lower operational costs.
- **Innovation and Competitive Advantage**: Embracing circular economy principles drives innovation in product design and business models, giving companies a competitive edge.
- **Brand Enhancement**: Companies that adopt circular economy practices often see an enhancement in their brand image, as they are perceived as responsible and forward-thinking.
- **Compliance and Risk Mitigation**: Adhering to circular economy principles can help businesses stay ahead of regulatory changes and reduce their exposure to resource scarcity and price volatility.

The Future Outlook

As we progress into the 22nd century, the circular economy will likely become essential to business strategy. By embracing its principles, businesses can contribute to a more sustainable world and unlock new opportunities for growth, innovation, and long-term success. The circular economy is not just an environmental imperative; it's a new way of thinking about business that is restorative, regenerative, and aligned with the future.

Chapter 4

DIGITAL TRANSFORMATION AND TECHNOLOGY INTEGRATION

Harnessing AI and Machine Learning

The advent of Artificial Intelligence (AI) and Machine Learning (ML) has revolutionized the way businesses operate, offering unprecedented opportunities for efficiency, innovation, and customer engagement. This section explores how AI and ML can be harnessed to transform various aspects of a home business.

- **Automating Routine Tasks**: AI can automate repetitive and time-consuming tasks, freeing entrepreneurs to focus on strategic planning and creative problem-solving.

- **Enhanced Customer Experiences**: AI-driven chatbots and virtual assistants can provide 24/7 customer service, while ML algorithms offer customers personalized product recommendations and experiences.
- **Data-Driven Insights**: ML algorithms analyze large datasets to extract actionable insights, aiding in informed decision-making and predictive analytics for market trends and customer behavior.
- **Optimizing Operations**: AI can optimize logistics, inventory management, and supply chain operations, making the business more efficient and cost-effective.

Blockchain and Cryptocurrency in Business

Blockchain technology and cryptocurrencies are more than just buzzwords in the 22nd century; they are integral to modern business operations. This part of the chapter delves into their application in home businesses.

- **Enhanced Security and Transparency**: Blockchain's decentralized and immutable ledger provides enhanced security and transparency in transactions and record-keeping.
- **Smart Contracts**: These self-executing contracts, with the terms of the agreement directly written into lines of code, can automate and streamline various business processes.
- **Global Transactions**: Cryptocurrencies enable seamless international transactions without the need for traditional banking systems, fostering a more inclusive global economy.
- **Tokenization of Assets**: Blockchain allows tokenizing physical assets, making trading and managing assets digitally easier.

Internet of Things (IoT) and Smart Home Integration

IoT has transformed homes into interconnected ecosystems, offering significant benefits for home-based businesses.

- **Efficient Resource Management**: IoT devices can monitor and manage resources like electricity and water, leading to more efficient operations and cost savings.
- **Enhanced Productivity**: Smart home devices can create an optimal work environment with automated lighting, temperature control, and security systems.
- **Data Collection and Analysis**: IoT devices provide valuable data that can be analyzed to improve business processes, understand customer preferences, and predict market trends.
- **Remote Monitoring and Management**: IoT enables entrepreneurs to remotely monitor and manage various aspects of their business, enhancing flexibility and responsiveness.

Conclusion

This chapter underscores the importance of digital transformation and technology integration in 21st-century home businesses. By embracing AI, blockchain, cryptocurrency, and IoT, entrepreneurs can streamline their operations and provide enhanced customer value, setting the stage for growth and success in an increasingly digital world.

Financial Planning and Management

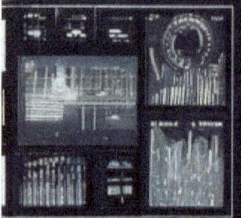
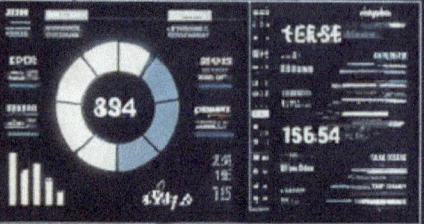

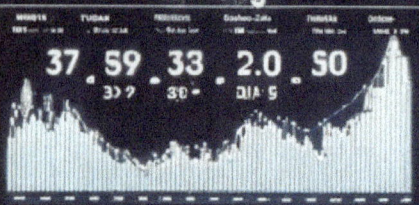

Chapter 5

FINANCIAL PLANNING AND MANAGEMENT

Budgeting and Financial Forecasting

Effective financial management begins with robust budgeting and forecasting. This section delves into the art and science of predicting future financial needs and managing current resources wisely.

- **Creating a Comprehensive Budget**: Learn how to develop a detailed budget that includes all aspects of your business operations, from startup costs to recurring expenses.
- **Revenue Forecasting**: Techniques for accurately forecasting sales and revenue, considering market trends, seasonal fluctuations, and historical data.

- **Expense Tracking**: Strategies for monitoring and controlling expenses, ensuring that the business stays within budget and operates efficiently.
- **Cash Flow Management**: Understanding the nuances of cash flow, including how to manage accounts receivable and payable to maintain healthy liquidity.

Innovative Financing and Investment Strategies

The landscape of financing and investment has evolved, offering new avenues for securing funds and investing capital.

- **Crowdfunding and Peer-to-Peer Lending**: Exploring modern fundraising methods such as crowdfunding platforms and peer-to-peer lending, which can provide alternative sources of capital.
- **Equity Financing**: Insights into equity financing options, including venture capital and angel investors, and how to attract and negotiate with these investors.

- **Cryptocurrency and Digital Investments**: Understanding the role of digital currencies and assets in raising capital and diversifying investments.
- **Sustainable and Ethical Investing**: The growing trend of ESG (Environmental, Social, and Governance) investing and how to align your investment strategies with sustainable and ethical practices.

Risk Management and Mitigation

Risk is inherent in any business venture, but managing and mitigating these risks is crucial for long-term success.

- **Identifying Potential Risks**: A guide to identifying various risks - financial, operational, market, and environmental - that your home business might face.
- **Developing a Risk Management Plan**: Steps to create a comprehensive plan to address potential risks, including contingency plans and risk mitigation strategies.

- **Insurance and Protection**: Information on various types of business insurance policies and how to choose the right coverage to protect your business from unforeseen events.
- **Building Resilience**: Tips for building a resilient business capable of withstanding financial shocks and market volatility.

Conclusion

This chapter delves into a home business's critical financial planning and management aspects in the 22nd century. From establishing a sound budgeting practice to exploring innovative financing options and effectively managing risks, this chapter equips entrepreneurs with the knowledge and tools necessary for sound financial health and long-term business sustainability.

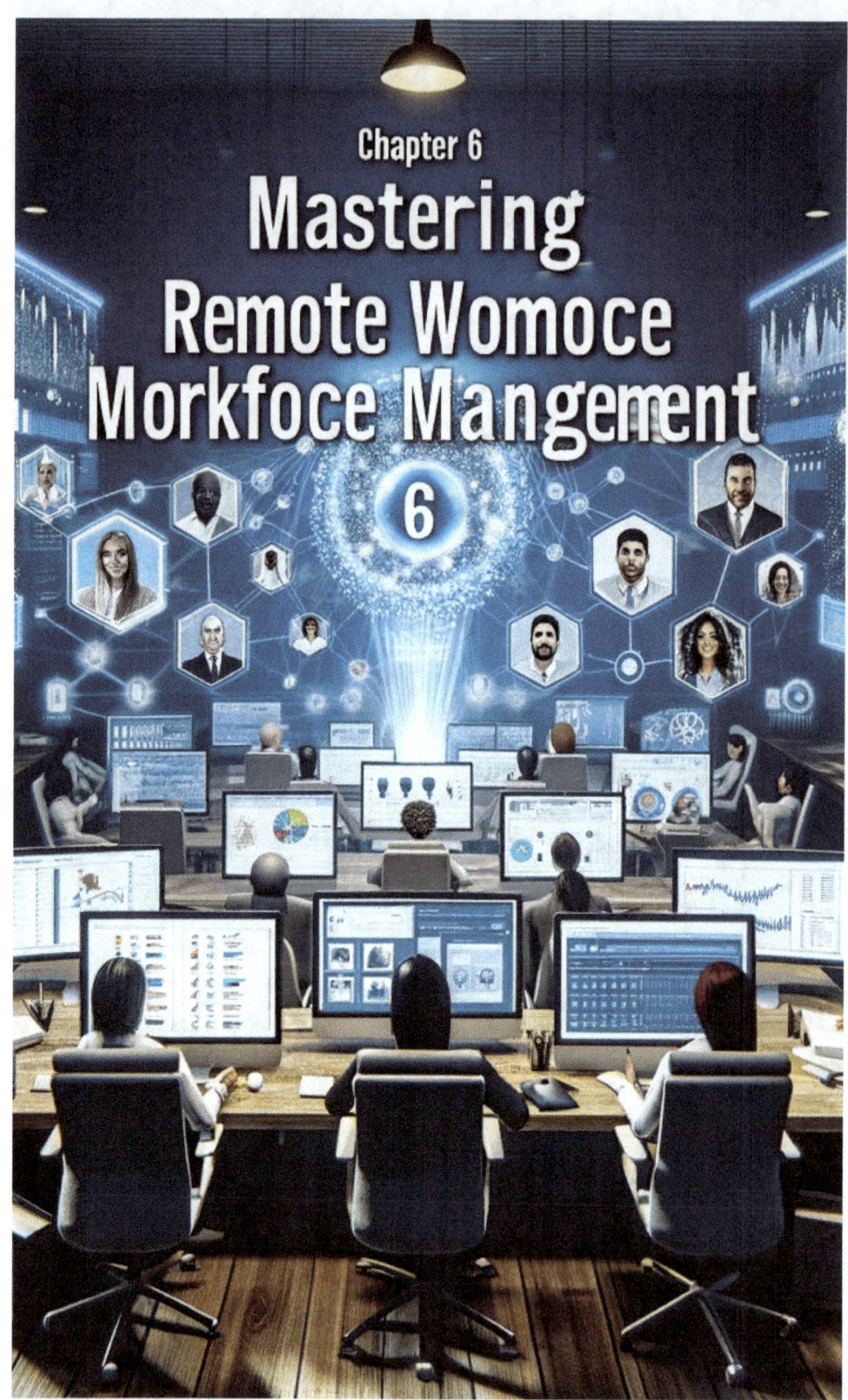

Chapter 6

MASTERING REMOTE WORKFORCE MANAGEMENT

The 22nd century has seen a paradigm shift in the workforce, with remote working becoming a norm rather than an exception. This chapter provides insights and strategies for effectively managing a remote team, ensuring productivity, and fostering a positive work culture.

Building and Managing a Remote Team

- **Recruitment and Onboarding**: Guidance on sourcing and hiring the best talent from a global pool and strategies for effective remote onboarding to integrate new team members seamlessly.

- **Setting Clear Expectations**: The importance of establishing clear goals, roles, and responsibilities to ensure everyone is on the same page.
- **Performance Management**: Techniques for monitoring and evaluating remote employees' performance, including setting up key performance indicators (KPIs) and regular check-ins.
- **Cultural Diversity and Inclusion**: Embracing diversity in a remote team and creating an inclusive environment that respects and values different perspectives and backgrounds.

Cultivating a Strong Company Culture Remotely

- **Defining Company Values**: How to define and communicate your company's values and mission in a way that resonates with remote employees.
- **Building Trust and Morale**: Strategies to build trust among team members and maintain high

morale, including recognizing achievements and celebrating milestones.

- **Fostering Team Connectivity**: Tips for creating a sense of belonging and community among remote workers, such as virtual team-building activities and informal meet-ups.

Effective Communication and Collaboration Tools

- **I am selecting the Right Tools**: Overview of the various communication and collaboration tools available for remote teams, including project management software, instant messaging apps, and video conferencing tools.
- **Best Practices for Digital Communication**: Guidelines for effective and efficient digital communication, including regular team meetings, one-on-one check-ins, and clear communication protocols.
- **Collaboration and Workflow Management**: Techniques to ensure smooth collaboration and workflow among team members, including shared calendars, task management systems, and document-sharing platforms.

Conclusion

Mastering remote workforce management is crucial in the 22nd century's business landscape. This chapter equips entrepreneurs with the necessary knowledge and tools to build, manage, and sustain a productive and cohesive remote team. By implementing these strategies, businesses can leverage the benefits of a diverse, global workforce while maintaining a solid company culture and ensuring effective communication and collaboration.

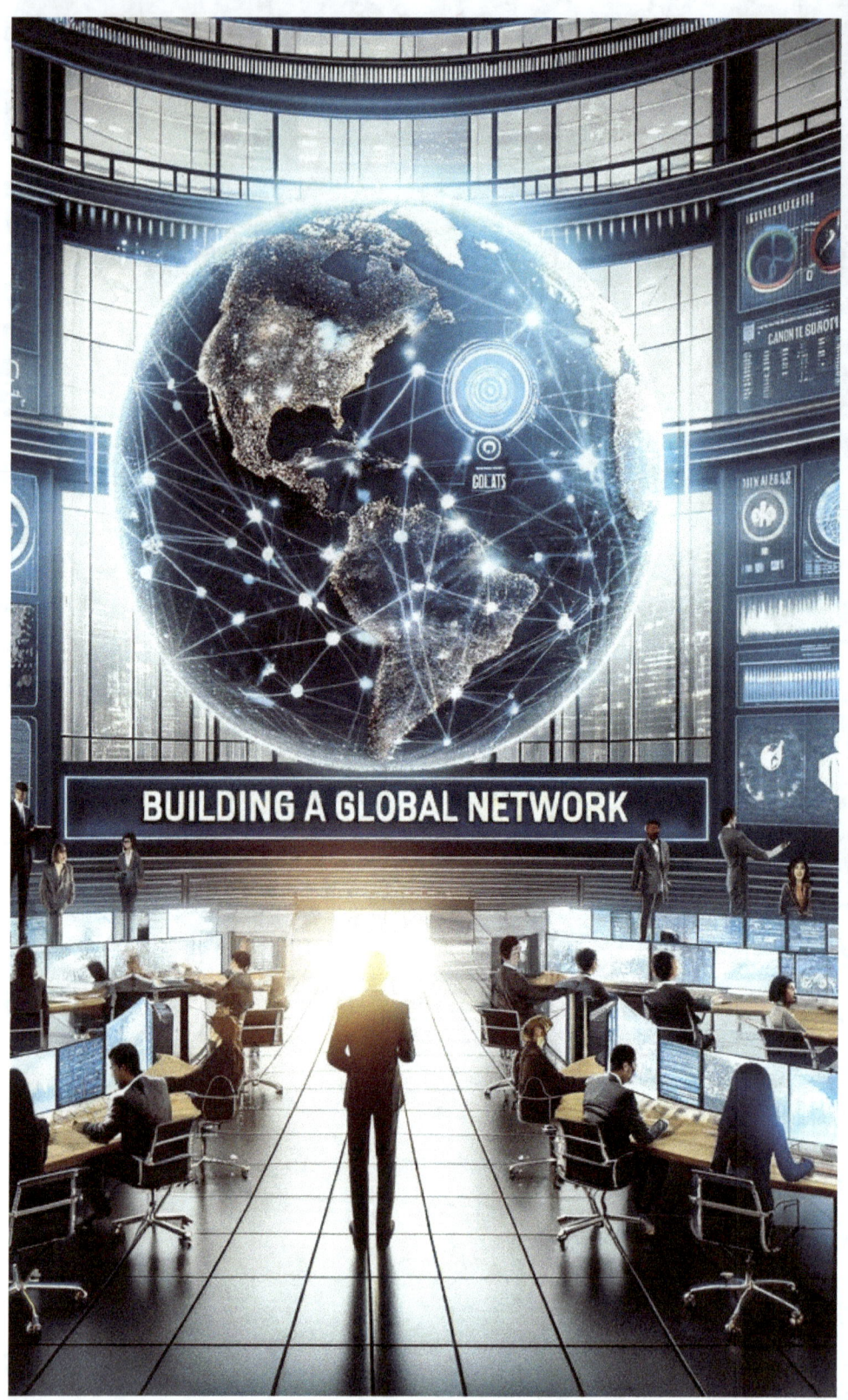

Chapter 7

BUILDING A GLOBAL NETWORK

In the interconnected world of the 22nd century, building a global network is essential for business expansion, innovation, and sustainability. This chapter delves into effective networking strategies, collaboration across borders, and navigating the complexities of international business relationships.

Networking in the Digital Era

- **Leveraging Digital Platforms**: An exploration of how to use social media, professional networking sites, and online forums to build and expand your business network.

- **Virtual Networking Events**: Tips for attending and making the most of virtual trade shows, webinars, and industry conferences.
- **Personal Branding Online**: Strategies for creating and maintaining a solid personal brand that resonates with a global audience, including content creation and digital storytelling.
- Collaborating and Partnering Across Borders
- **Finding the Right Partners**: Guidance on identifying and connecting with potential business partners, suppliers, and collaborators worldwide.
- **Cross-Border Collaboration Models**: Various models of international collaboration, including joint ventures, strategic alliances, and outsourcing partnerships.
- **Legal and Financial Considerations**: Key legal and financial aspects to consider when forming international partnerships, such as contracts, intellectual property rights, and taxation.

Navigating Cultural Differences in Business

- **Cultural Intelligence**: Understanding the importance of cultural intelligence in international business and tips for developing it.
- **Communication Across Cultures**: Techniques for effective communication that respect and adapt to cultural nuances, including language barriers and non-verbal cues.
- **Building Trust and Rapport**: Strategies for building long-lasting business relationships across different cultures, focusing on respect, empathy, and understanding.

Conclusion

Building a global network in the 22nd century requires combining digital savvy, cultural intelligence, and strategic thinking. This chapter provides a comprehensive guide to navigating the digital landscape for networking, collaborating across diverse cultures, and establishing strong international partnerships. By embracing these practices, businesses can expand their horizons, tap into new markets, and thrive in the global economy.

Chapter 8

CUSTOMER ENGAGEMENT AND RETENTION

In the dynamic market of the 22nd century, engaging and retaining customers is crucial for the sustained success of any business. This chapter explores innovative strategies for creating personalized customer experiences, developing loyalty programs, and leveraging social media and online communities.

Creating Personalized Customer Experiences

- **Understanding Your Customer**: The importance of gathering and analyzing customer data to gain insights into their preferences and behaviors.

- **Customization and Personalization**: Strategies for using technology to create customized and personalized experiences that cater to individual customer needs and preferences.
- **Technology in Personalization**: How AI and machine learning can personalize marketing messages, product recommendations, and customer interactions.
- Loyalty Programs and Customer Feedback Loops
- **We are designing Effective Loyalty Programs**: Tips for creating loyalty programs that genuinely add value to customers and encourage repeat business.
- **Integrating Feedback Mechanisms**: Incorporating customer feedback loops into your business model to continually improve products and services.
- **We are analyzing and Acting on Feedback**: Techniques for analyzing customer feedback

and using the insights gained to make informed business decisions and enhancements.

- Utilizing Social Media and Online Communities
- **Building a Strong Social Media Presence**: Best practices for using various social media platforms to engage with customers and build brand awareness.
- **Creating Online Communities**: Strategies for building and nurturing online communities around your brand, including forums, social media groups, and interactive platforms.
- **Engagement through Content**: How to create compelling, relevant, and engaging content that resonates with your target audience and fosters a sense of community.

Conclusion

Customer engagement and retention are more critical than ever in the 22nd century's competitive business landscape. This chapter equips businesses with the necessary tools and strategies to create personalized experiences, foster customer loyalty, and leverage digital platforms for ongoing engagement. Businesses can achieve long-term success and a loyal customer base by prioritizing customer satisfaction and building strong relationships.

Chapter 9

STAYING AHEAD OF THE CURVE

In the rapidly evolving business environment of the 22nd century, they are staying relevant and competitive and demand constant adaptation and innovation. This chapter focuses on the importance of continuous learning, adaptability to market changes, and the cultivation of innovation.

Continuous Learning and Skill Development

- **Lifelong Learning Mindset**: Emphasizing adopting a mindset geared towards continuous learning and development.

- **Skill Upgradation**: Identifying and acquiring new skills in demand, particularly those related to emerging technologies and market trends.
- **Utilizing Educational Resources**: Leveraging online courses, webinars, workshops, and other educational resources to stay updated and skilled.
- Adapting to Market Changes and Challenges
- **Market Trend Analysis**: Techniques for keeping a pulse on market trends and customer preferences using tools like big data analytics and market research.
- **Flexibility in Business Models**: The ability to adapt business models to market shifts, technological advancements, and consumer behavior changes.
- **Crisis Management**: Preparing for and effectively managing business crises, including developing contingency plans and maintaining operational flexibility.

Innovating and Pioneering New Ideas

- **Fostering a Culture of Innovation**: Creating a business culture that encourages creativity, experimentation, and new ideas.
- **Technological Advancements as Catalysts**: Utilizing cutting-edge technologies to drive innovation in products, services, and business processes.
- **Collaborative Innovation**: Embracing collaboration with other businesses, researchers, and innovators to combine strengths and foster groundbreaking ideas.

Conclusion

Staying ahead of the curve in the 22nd century requires an unrelenting commitment to learning, adaptability, and innovation. This chapter provides a roadmap for businesses to cultivate these essential qualities, ensuring they survive and thrive in a constantly changing business landscape. By embracing change and fostering a culture of continuous improvement and innovation, businesses can secure their place at the forefront of their industries.

Conclusion

NAVIGATING THE FUTURE OF HOME BUSINESS

As we stand at the threshold of new business horizons, the future of home business in the 22nd century presents a landscape brimming with possibilities and challenges. This book, "22nd Century Home Business Strategy Blueprint," has journeyed through the various facets of building and sustaining a home business in this dynamic era, emphasizing the importance of adaptation, innovation, and resilience.

The Future of Home Business

The future is a realm of endless opportunities for home businesses. With the advancements in technology and the shift in global economic patterns, home businesses have the potential to reach unparalleled heights. This new era will see home businesses not just surviving but thriving, breaking traditional boundaries, and setting new benchmarks of success.

Embracing Change and Pursuing Growth

One of the key takeaways from this journey is the importance of embracing change. In a world where change is the only constant, flexibility, and adaptability are not just assets but necessities. Entrepreneurs must be willing to evolve, learn, and grow continuously. By staying attuned to technological advancements, market trends, and shifting consumer behaviors, home businesses can adapt to change and anticipate and lead it.

Final Thoughts and Encouragement for Entrepreneurs

To all aspiring and established entrepreneurs, this conclusion serves as a beacon of encouragement and a reminder of the potential within each of you. The road ahead may be peppered with challenges, but it is also laden with opportunities for growth, innovation, and success.

Remember, the journey of entrepreneurship is as rewarding as the destination. Each challenge you face is an opportunity to learn, and each failure is a stepping stone to success. Embrace the journey with passion, resilience, and an unwavering belief in your vision.

As you read this book and embark on your entrepreneurial journey, carry the insights, strategies, and lessons it imparts. Let them guide you as you navigate the exciting and ever-evolving world of home business in the 22nd century.

Ultimately, the future belongs to those who believe in the beauty of their dreams. Go forth and build the future you envision, armed with knowledge, driven by innovation, and inspired by the endless possibilities that await.

Welcome to the future of home business. Your journey starts now.

Case Studies

CASE STUDIES OF SUCCESSFUL 22ND-CENTURY HOME BUSINESSES

Case Study 1: Ecotec Home Solutions

Background: Ecotec Home Solutions, started in 2205, is a business that combines AI-driven technology with sustainable living solutions. They design and sell innovative, eco-friendly home systems that monitor and manage energy usage, waste production, and water conservation.

Challenge: The challenge was to create a product that resonated with environmentally conscious consumers while ensuring seamless integration with the latest smart home technology.

Solution: EcoTech developed a range of IoT-enabled devices that homeowners could control via a central AI system. These devices included solar-powered heating systems, AI-managed recycling units, and water-saving appliances.

Outcome: The business saw a rapid growth in sales, particularly in urban areas where environmental impact and energy savings were significant concerns. EcoTech's ability to merge technology with sustainability proved to be a major market differentiator.

Case Study 2: Virtual Learning Hub

Background: In 2210, Virtual Learning Hub began as a small home business providing online tutoring services using VR and AR technologies.

Challenge: The challenge was to provide a personalized and immersive learning experience that could rival traditional in-person tutoring.

Solution: The company utilized VR and AR to create interactive, 3D learning environments for students.

They also employed AI algorithms to adapt teaching styles and content based on individual student performance and feedback.

Outcome: The Virtual Learning Hub quickly became a popular alternative to conventional tutoring, with students reporting higher levels of engagement and understanding. The business expanded its services globally, capitalizing on the need for more geographical constraints in the digital realm.

Case Study 3: Health at Home

Background: Health at Home, started in 2215, specializes in telemedicine and home health monitoring, providing remote healthcare services.

Challenge: The challenge was to offer comprehensive healthcare services remotely, ensuring accuracy, privacy, and ease of use for patients with varying levels of technological proficiency.

Solution: The business developed an integrated telemedicine platform using advanced diagnostics, AI-driven health assessments, and secure video conferencing for consultations. They also offered easy-to-use health monitoring devices for patients to use at home.

Outcome: Health at Home saw a surge in demand, especially from elderly and immobile patients who found it challenging to visit healthcare facilities. The company's emphasis on user-friendly design and robust data security helped it become a trusted name in home healthcare.

Conclusion

These case studies showcase the potential and diversity of home businesses in the 22nd century. Each illustrates the importance of innovative solutions, technological integration, and adaptability to market needs. They serve as inspiring examples for entrepreneurs looking to carve their niche in the evolving landscape of home business.

Resource List

TOOLS, TECHNOLOGIES, AND PLATFORMS FOR 22ND CENTURY HOME BUSINESSES

Business Management and Productivity

Asana: Advanced project management tool for task assignments, timelines, and progress tracking.

Trello: Visual tool for organizing and prioritizing projects using boards, lists, and cards.

Slack: Communication platform that integrates with multiple tools for team collaboration.

Zoom: Video conferencing tool essential for remote meetings and webinars.

Microsoft Teams: Collaboration platform that combines chat, video meetings, file storage, and integration with other Microsoft Office apps.

Marketing and Customer Relationship Management

HubSpot: Comprehensive inbound marketing, sales, and service software.

Mailchimp: Email marketing platform with automation, analytics, and audience segmentation capabilities.

Google Analytics: Essential tool for website traffic analysis and digital marketing insights.

Hootsuite: Social media management platform for scheduling posts, monitoring conversations, and analyzing social media traffic.

Financial Management

QuickBooks: Accounting software for small businesses, offering invoicing, expense tracking, and payroll functions.

FreshBooks: Cloud-based accounting software known for its ease of use, particularly in invoicing and time tracking.

Wave: Free financial software for small businesses, offering accounting, invoicing, and receipt scanning.

E-Commerce and Sales

Shopify: E-commerce platform for setting up an online store, managing inventory, and processing payments.

Etsy: Online marketplace for selling unique, handmade, or vintage items.

Square: Payment processing tool that offers solutions for e-commerce, point-of-sale, and business analytics.

Technology and Innovation

GitHub: Platform for software development and version control using Git, enabling collaboration among developers.

Arduino: Open-source electronic prototyping platform for creating interactive electronic objects.

Raspberry Pi: Small, affordable computer for learning programming and digital making.

Design and Creativity

Adobe Creative Cloud: Suite of software for graphic design, video editing, web development, and photography.

Canva: User-friendly graphic design tool with templates for social media graphics, presentations, posters, and more.

Sketch: Digital design toolkit for UI/UX design focusing on-screen design.

Research and Development

Google Scholar: Search engine for academic literature across various disciplines.

Mendeley: Reference manager and academic social network that helps organize research, collaborate with others, and discover the latest research.

Remote Work and Collaboration

VPN Services: Tools like NordVPN or ExpressVPN for secure and remote access to business networks.

Dropbox: Cloud storage service for file sharing and collaboration.

TeamViewer: Remote control, desktop sharing, and file transfer software that works behind any firewall and NAT proxy.

Conclusion

This comprehensive list of tools, technologies, and platforms is designed to equip 22nd-century home business owners with the resources to effectively manage, grow, and innovate their businesses in a digital and interconnected world.

www.ingramcontent.com/pod-product-compliance
Lightning Source LLC
Chambersburg PA
CBHW062352290526
45794CB00005B/2188